# Twenty to Make
# Eco-Friendly Knits

## Using Recycled Plastic Bags

### Emily Blades

Search Press

First published in Great Britain 2010

Search Press Limited
Wellwood, North Farm Road,
Tunbridge Wells, Kent TN2 3DR

Reprinted 2011

Text copyright © Emily Blades 2010

Photographs by Debbie Patterson at
Search Press studios

Photographs and design copyright
© Search Press Ltd 2010

ISBN: 978-1-84448-486-7

### Suppliers

If you have difficulty in obtaining any of the
materials and equipment mentioned in this book,
then please visit the Search Press website for
details of suppliers: www.searchpress.com

Printed in Malaysia.

*Dedication*
*For my parents who taught me so well,*
*my husband who supports me in all I*
*do, my darling twins for putting up with*
*my obsession with knitting. And last but*
*not least Gerard Allt for enabling me to*
*believe in myself.*

## Abbreviations

**beg:** beginning

**dec:** decrease (by working two
stitches together)

**g st:** garter stitch (knit every row)

**inc:** increase (by working into the front and
back of the stitch)

**k:** knit

**k2tog:** knit two stitches together

**p:** purl

**p2tog:** purl two stitches together

**rib:** ribbing (one stitch knit, one stitch purl)

**st:** stitch(es)

**st st:** stocking stitch (one row knit, one
row purl)

**\*-\*\*:** Repeat from the point marked * to the
point marked **

# Contents

# Introduction

I am very excited to bring you the first ever book on knitting and recycling, a craft that came about quite by chance for me. After reading about knitting with strips of plastic cut from shopping bags, I was inspired to create unique and desirable objects that are pleasing to look at, useful and also help the environment by cutting down on waste plastic.

Throughout this book I refer to the plastic as 'plarn' – a combination of the words plastic and yarn. It is very satisfying to end up with balls of colourful plarn instead of a dustbin full of disused bags!

The projects in this book range from beginner to advanced, so whatever your knitting ability you will be sure to find something to make. All the items would make excellent gifts with the smaller ones easily done for those last-minute occasions. I hope you have as much fun knitting them as I have had designing them all!

*Emily Blades*

## Preparing Plarn

These step-by-step instructions show how to make the plarn used throughout the book from average-weight plastic bags. This will knit up to an approximate double knit tension.

Thinner bags are easier to work with, so use those when you start out. The thinnest, flimsiest bags should be cut into wider strips of 4cm (1½in), and the heaviest, most glossy bags should be trimmed into narrower 1cm (¾in) strips for the same tension.

Plastic bags of one colour will let you make items with solid colour, but you can make variegated plarn from striped or patterned bags.

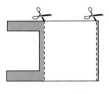 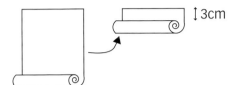 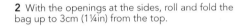  

↕ 3cm

**1** Lay a clean, dry plastic bag out flat and cut off the sealed bottom and handles, leaving you with a cylinder shape.

**2** With the openings at the sides, roll and fold the bag up to 3cm (1¼in) from the top.

**3** Using scissors, cut the folded part only, into strips approximately 2cm (1in) wide.

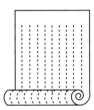 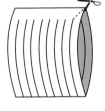 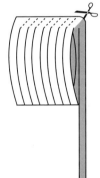 

**4** Unroll the cylinder and you will have a lot of single loops hanging from the uncut part of the bag.

**5** Open the bag out and slip the scissors under the uncut part of the bag. Make a cut diagonally from the outside edge of the bag to the top of the first inside loop, on the side facing you only.

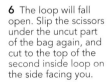

**6** The loop will fall open. Slip the scissors under the uncut part of the bag again, and cut to the top of the second inside loop on the side facing you.

**7** Continue cutting in this way until all the strips are separated. You should now have one long continuous strip of plastic.

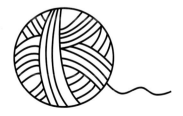

**8** Roll the strip up into a ball. You now have a ball of plarn that is ready to be used for knitting!

# Mobile Phone Sock

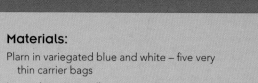

## Materials:

Plarn in variegated blue and white – five very
  thin carrier bags

Large darning needle

## Needles:

1 pair 4mm (UK 8; US 6) knitting needles

## Instructions:

### Knitting
Cast on 40st and knit in k1, p1 rib for 8 rows. Continue in stocking stitch until the work measures 12cm (4¾in). Cast off.

### Making up
Sew in any unwanted ends then fold the work in half, with the wrong side on the outside. Thread some spare plarn on to your darning needle and stitch together the sides and bottom of the sock (see detail opposite).

Turn the piece the right way out and your mobile sock is ready to use.

### Tweed Look
*Those flimsy, striped bags from the corner shop are ideal for this project.*

# Purse

## Materials:

Plarn in purple, pink and black – approximately
  one carrier bag of each colour

Large darning needle

Sewing needle and thread

A 10cm (4in) zip

## Needles:

1 pair 3.75mm (UK 9; US 5) knitting needles

## Instructions:

Work in stocking stitch throughout.

### Knitting

Cast on 25st. Starting with a knit row, work 2 rows in purple. * Work 1 row pink, 2 rows black, 1 row pink, 5 rows purple, 1 row black, 2 rows pink, 1 row black, 5 rows purple **. Repeat from * to ** until work measures 23cm (9in). Cast off.

### Making up

Fold the work in two and sew the cast-on edge to the cast-off edge. Turn the work sideways and stitch up the bottom of the work (this is actually the side of the knitting). This ensures that your stripes are running vertically rather than horizontally.

Oversew these seams with plarn on the right side out. Insert the zip into the opening at the top and discreetly stitch in place with sewing thread. For the zip pull (see detail opposite), thread two strips of plarn through the hole in the zip pull, making sure the plarn is of even lengths. Plait and knot it in place.

### Green Lines

*Try using natural colours for a more mature look.*

# Belt

**Materials:**

Plarn in silver – two foil bread bags; and black –
    two or three black bin liners
Darning and sewing needles and thread
One buckle

**Needles:**

1 pair 3.75mm (UK 9; US 5)
    knitting needles

## Instructions:

### Knitting
Cast on 10st with black plarn. Rows 1-5 stocking stitch. Row 6 garter (this forms the edge of turn over). Rows 7–14 work in moss stitch (also known as seed stitch). Row 15 * k1, p1, k1, join in silver k4, join in black p1, k1, p1. Row 16, with the black, p1, k1, p1, with the silver k4, then k1, p1, k1 in black. Repeat the last 2 rows 3 times. With black k1, p1, k5, p1, k1, p1. Carry on in moss stitch for 9 more rows **. Repeat from * to ** until the belt is the desired length, ending on a right side row. K1 row in garter stitch; this forms an edge for stitching over the buckle bar. Work 10 rows in stocking stitch starting with a knit row. Cast off.

### Making up
Sew in any unwanted plarn. Fold over the cast-on edge at the garter row and stitch in place with sewing thread. At the cast-off end, thread the work over the bar of the buckle and fold at the point of the garter row (see detail opposite). Sew in place with thread.

### The finished piece
*This glitzy belt would make the perfect accessory to brighten any outfit.*

# Bead Earrings

## Materials:

Plarn in cool pink, lilac and hot pink –
  small amounts

6 small beads

Sewing needle and thread

Jewellery findings: Pair of earring hooks

## Needles:

1 pair 3.75mm (UK 9; US 5) knitting needles

## Instructions:

### Knitting

Cast on 6 st in plarn of your colour choice.
Work in stocking stitch for 8 rows. Cast off.
Repeat five times.

### Making up

Run a gathering stitch along all four sides of
work and gather together, tucking in unused
ends as you go. This creates the knitted bead.
Secure the end discreetly.

Alternate 3 knitted beads with 3 small hard
beads and string together with thread, sewing
firmly in place.

Stitch this to the earring attachment (see detail
opposite). Now they are ready to wear. If you
make them in colours to match your outfit, you
will have a very special and unique accessory.

**Autumn Golds**
*These warm gold and ochre beads
are very flattering to all skin tones.*

# Drink Mats

## Materials:

Plarn in blue and pink – approximately one
  carrier bag of each colour

Darning needle

An iron and ironing board

Baking parchment or greaseproof paper

## Needles:

1 pair 3.75mm (UK 9; US 5) knitting needles

## Instructions:

This project is simple enough for a child to do, but it needs adult supervision as part of the process involves a hot iron.

### Knitting

Cast on 25 st. Work in garter stitch throughout. Work 2 rows in blue plarn. Next knit 5st in blue, then join in pink plarn and knit 15st. Knit last 5st in blue. Repeat this row 28 times. Now using blue plarn only, work 2 rows. Cast off. You can adjust the number of rows you do to alter the size of the finished piece.

### Making up

Sew in any unwanted ends. Heat an iron to the hottest setting. Make sure an adult helps with this part. Place the knitting between two pieces of baking parchment. (This is vital unless you want a sticky mess on your iron!) Press and hold the iron firmly on to the paper and knitting for approximately twenty seconds. This melts the plastic enough to fuse it together and yet does not obliterate the pattern (see detail opposite).

Turn the work and paper over and repeat the heating process on the other side. Do not touch it until it has cooled down. When completely cold, it will be rigid and ready to use.

## Planets and Stripes

*Once your mats have cooled, they can be cut into circles with scissors.*

# Hair Bands with Bobbles

## Materials:
Plarn in red, white and blue – small amounts
Plain undecorated elastic hair band
Darning and sewing needles and thread

## Needles:
1 pair 3.75mm (UK 9; US 5) knitting needles

## Instructions:

### Knitting
Cast on 6 st. Work 8 rows in garter stitch.
Cast off.

### Making up
Run a gathering stitch with plarn along all four
sides and gather together, tucking in any plarn
ends as you go, thus moulding and forming a
bobble. Secure the plarn firmly in place.

   Arrange the bobbles to look pleasing, then
sew them on to the hair band with a fine needle
and sewing thread (see detail).

## Bobbles with Bling

*You can change the look easily by knitting in one colour or in stripes. For a more glamorous evening look, stitch on seed beads.*

# Travel Card Wallet

## Materials:

Plarn in pink, black, lime, and orange – approximately one carrier bag

Darning and sewing needles and thread

Two pins

## Needles:

1 pair 3.75mm (UK 9; US 5) knitting needles

## Instructions:

Work in stocking stitch throughout. It is a good idea to carry the colours up the side of the work as you go to save sewing in lots of ends afterwards.

### Knitting

Cast on 15 st. Knit 122 rows: colours as follows. 2 rows black, 4 rows pink, 2 rows black, 6 rows lime, 4 rows pink, 4 rows orange, 2 rows pink, 2 rows lime, 6 rows black, 4 rows orange, 6 rows pink, 6 rows black, 2 rows lime, 4 rows black, 6 rows orange, 2 rows lime, 4 rows orange, 2 rows pink, 2 rows lime, 6 rows black, 4 rows lime, 4 rows black, 4 rows lime, 4 rows pink, 2 rows black, 2 rows pink, 2 rows black, 4 rows pink, 4 rows orange, 2 rows pink, 2 rows lime, 6 rows black, 6 rows orange. Cast off.

### Making up

Sew in any unwanted ends of plarn. Fold work in half and mark the middle with the pins. Open the work flat and fold the cast-on and cast-off ends towards the pins. Leave approx 1cm (½in) between the two ends: i.e. 5mm (¼in) either side of the pins. This leaves a little gap and extra space for when the cards are inserted and the holder is folded in half (see detail opposite).

With the work inside-out, sew the side seams with the sewing thread, then turn work right way out. With plarn in a contrasting colour, use a whipping stitch to decorate the sides. This is solely cosmetic, and hides any cotton thread showing, producing a more finished look.

Now you are ready to insert cards, fold the wallet closed and use it! Finished size is approximately 10 x 7cm (4 x 2¾in).

### The finished piece

*Try combining blues and purples for a more masculine look.*

# Heart Necklace

**Materials:**

Plarn in red – one thick carrier bag; and silver –
one foil bread bag

Paper tissue

Darning needle, sewing needle and thread

Small glass beads

Nylon thread

Jewellery findings: Necklace fastening

**Needles:**

1 pair 4mm (UK 8; US 6) knitting needles

# Instructions:

## Beads

### Knitting and making up
Make 18 beads in silver plarn, following the instructions as for the Bead Earrings (see pages 12–13).

## Red heart

### Knitting
This is made in reversed stocking stitch. Cast on 2 st. Row 1 knit. Row 2 purl. Row 3 knit, increasing 1 stitch at each end of the row. Row 4 purl. Row 5 knit, increasing 1 stitch at each end of the row. Row 6 purl.

Continue increasing on every knit row until you have 10 stitches in all. Work 3 rows without any shaping. Next row decrease 1 stitch each end of the row. Purl next row. Knit and decrease as before on this row and every knit row until 2 stitches remain. Cast off.

### Making up
Fold the work in half, making a triangle with the smooth side on the inside, tucking any unwanted ends in. Stuff with paper tissue and sew up the sides using plarn.

Discreetly secure a strip of plarn at the point of the heart, and from the inside, catch the top centre of the triangle and pull downwards, towards the point, securing in place. This gives the triangle a heart shape (see detail opposite).

Thread the glass beads and knitted beads alternately on to the nylon thread with the heart at the centre. Knot the necklace fastenings to the ends. Now your necklace is ready to wear.

## Black and White Elegance
*No-one can have too much jewellery! Have fun making more necklaces in a variety of colours.*

# Disc Earrings

## Materials:

Plarn in purple and green – small amounts
Sewing needle and thread
10 small hard beads
Jewellery findings: Pair of earring hooks

## Needles:

1 pair 4mm (UK 8; US 6) knitting needles

# Instructions:

### Knitting

Cast on 20 st in green plarn and knit in stocking stitch for 3 rows. Change plarn colour to purple and continue in stocking stitch for another 4 rows. Cast off.

### Making up

With the work inside out, sew together the 2 ends of row edges. Run a gathering stitch along the cast-on edge of the work and pull it tight, securing it in place. Turn the work the right way out and run another gathering stitch along the cast-off row edge, pulling it in tight to secure.

Stitch the two middles together, thus making a small disc, green one side and purple the other. Place 2 beads either side of the disc in the middle and stitch in place (see detail opposite). Fasten thread at the top edge of the rim, and thread on 3 beads and an earring attachment. Make sure you run the thread back through the beads to secure them firmly.

## Raspberry Ripple

*These earrings can easily be knitted in an hour, so they would make an ideal last-minute gift or stocking filler.*

# Vase

## Materials:

Plarn in pink, lilac, brown and white –
approximately eight carrier bags

Empty and clean plastic drink bottle

Darning needle

Pair of scissors

## Needles:

1 pair 5mm (UK 6; US 8) knitting needles

## Instructions:

### Knitting

Cast on 46 stitches with pink plarn or colour of your choice. Row 1 k2, p2 along the whole row. Row 2 p2, k2 along the whole row. Repeat rows 1 and 2. Continue the rest of the work in stocking stitch, starting with a knit row, patterning as follows: 4 rows in lilac plarn, 2 rows in brown, 4 rows in pink, 8 rows in white, 2 rows in pink, 6 rows in lilac, 2 rows pink, 4 rows brown, 14 rows white, 4 rows lilac. Cast off. (Some of the bags I used had some writing on them, thus creating the flecks of colour.)

### Making up

Sew in any unwanted ends on the knitting. Join the side seams with plarn, inside out (see detail opposite). Then turn the correct side out.

Use the scissors to cut the top off the plastic bottle. Now slip the knitted sleeve over the top of the bottle and smooth it into place. It should be tight enough to stay in place but can easily be removed when the bottle requires cleaning.

### The finished piece

*This project can be done in any colours that complement the décor of the room (or garden!) in which it will be used.*

# MP3 Player Sleeve

**Materials:**

Plarn in variegated white and green –
  approximately one carrier bag

Darning needle

**Needles:**

1 pair 3.75mm (UK 9; US 5)
knitting needles

## Instructions:

### Knitting
Cast on 15 st. Work 4 rows in k1, p1, rib.
Change to stocking stitch and continue until
work measures 18cm (7in). Work 4 more rows in
k1, p1, rib and cast off.

### Making up
Fold work together so that the two ribbings are
at the top (see detail opposite) and oversew
the side seams in plarn.

## Funky Stripes

*These are very easy to knit, so would be perfect for
children to make. Let them choose and collect their
own plastic bags in order to make their finished
piece personal and unique.*

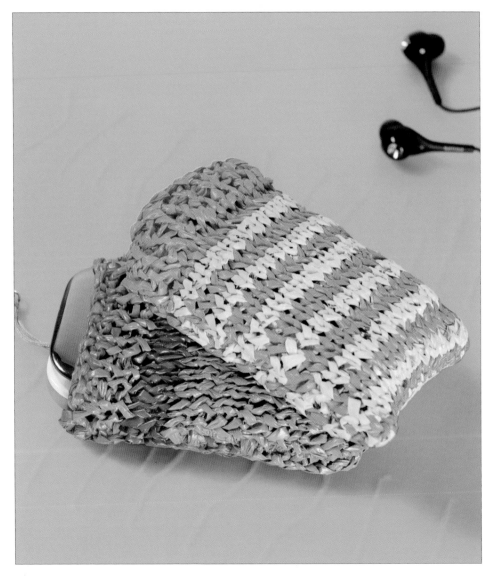

# Brooch

**Materials:**

Plarn in yellow, green and orange –
  small amounts of each

Darning and sewing needles and thread

Jewellery findings: Brooch pin

**Needles:**

1 pair 2.75mm (UK 12; US 2) knitting needles

## Instructions:

### Knitting
### For the flower

With yellow plarn cast on 33 st. Knit 1 row. Purl 1 row. Next row knit 5 st, turn, * p5 turn, k5 turn, p5 turn, decrease 1 st at each end of next row and turn, p3 turn, decrease 1 st at beginning of the row, knit the remaining stitch, turn, p2 turn, k2tog and fasten off. The first petal is complete.

Rejoin plarn to main work and cast off next 2 st then k4, thus having 5 st on your right-hand needle **. Follow instructions from * to ** until all 33 stitches have been worked. Sew in any loose ends. Pick up and knit 18 st along the 33 st cast-on edge. Next row purl. Next row k1, slip1, k1, pass the slip stitch over, repeat this to the end. Starting with a purl row, work 8 rows in stocking stitch. Cast off.

### For the first leaf

With green plarn, cast on 3 st. Work in stocking stitch until work measures 8cm (3¼in) ending on a knit row. Cast off 1 st at the beginning of the next row. Work 6 more rows in st st. Cast off.

### For the second leaf

With green plarn cast on 3 st. Work in stocking stitch for 4cm (1½in) ending on a purl row. Cast off 1 st at the beginning of the next row. Work 6 more rows. Cast off.

### For the stalk

With orange plarn cast on 5 st and work 8 rows in stocking stitch. Change to green plarn and continue in stocking stitch until work measures 11cm (4¼in). Cast off.

### Making up

Join the side seam of the flower's trumpet. Join the side seam of the stalk. Insert the orange tip of the stalk into the back of the trumpet and stitch in place. Position the leaves on the stalk and stitch them in place using plarn of matching colour. With sewing thread and a fine needle, stitch or fasten the brooch pin to the back of the flower (see detail opposite).

## The finished piece

*This delightful daffodil will be adored by all who see it. Why not give one to the gardener in your life?*

# Desk Tidy

## Materials:

Plarn in light purple, dark purple, pink and
  dark blue – approximately one carrier
  bag of each colour; and light blue –
  approximately two carrier bags

Clean and empty 1 litre yogurt pot

Darning needle

## Needles:

1 pair 5mm (UK 6; US 8) knitting needles

## Instructions:

### Knitting
Cast on 70 st. Knit in garter stitch for 5 rows. Then change to stocking stitch working straight until work measures 14cm (5½in). Cast off.

### Making up
Oversew the side seam the right way out using plarn. Slip over the pot and thread a running stitch along the cast-on edge. Gently pull tight, allowing the edge to cover the lip of the pot (see detail opposite). Secure and oversew the rim edge.

### The finished piece
*The different shades of plarn even within one colour make each piece individual and unique. Have fun experimenting!*

# Waste Paper Basket

## Materials:

Plarn in red, yellow, green, blue, indigo and violet –
approximately eighteen carrier bags altogether

Darning needle

Baking parchment or greaseproof paper

An iron

A metal bin, wicker basket or toughened plastic
container over which you can mould the knitted bin

## Needles:

1 pair 5mm (UK 6; US 8) knitting needles

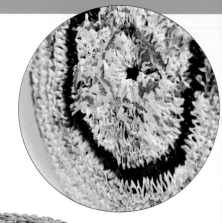

## Instructions:

This project is simple enough for a child to do, but it requires adult supervision as part of the process involves using an iron.

### Knitting

Cast on 90 st. Work in garter stitch until work measures 35cm (13¾in) or desired height. Cast off.

### Making up

Sew in unwanted ends and join the side seam using matching plarn. Thread a running stitch along the cast-off edge and pull tight, securing firmly. You may find it easier to use a little nylon thread for this. Place the knitted bin over your 'mould'. Place baking parchment between the mould and your knitting as well as between the knitting and the iron! (This is essential if you want to avoid getting a plastic mess all over your iron.)

Heat the iron to the hottest setting and hold for a few seconds against the gathered up base until it is flattened and fused together (see detail opposite). Then slowly iron all around the outside of the bin. While the knitting is warm it will appear soft and floppy but once it has cooled it will be firm enough to keep its shape and stand up. You have now recycled your rubbish to hold more litter.

### The finished piece

*This waste paper basket is a favourite of mine. Every room can benefit from one and I use colours to match the decor.*

# Building Blocks

## Materials:

Plarn in orange, yellow and cream – approximately
   three standard-sized carrier bags of each colour

Darning needle

Soft toy filler or spare plastic bags

## Needles:

1 pair 4mm (UK 8; US 6) knitting needles

## Instructions:

### Knitting

Cast on 15 st. Work in garter stitch throughout. Work 23 rows or as many as it takes to produce a square. Cast off. Make 6 of these squares in all.

### Making up

Oversew the squares together to form a block. Leave one side open to fill with stuffing, and then sew the last square in place. Make sure all seams are secure so that the filling cannot be pulled out by little hands or paws!

### Toys

*It is not only children who enjoy playing with these soft blocks. Pets also love chasing after them and knocking them down!*

# Bottle Holder

## Materials:

Variegated plarn in green and black – approximately two
very large plastic bags

Darning needle

Baking parchment or greaseproof paper

A clean and empty food tin

An iron

## Needles:

1 pair 5.5mm (UK 5; US 9)
knitting needles

## Instructions:

This project is simple enough for a child to do, but it needs adult supervision as part of the process involves using an iron.

### Knitting

Cast on 70 st. Knit in garter stitch for 5 rows. Then change to stocking stitch, working straight until work measures 14cm (5½in). Cast off.

### Making up

Oversew side seam the right way out. Slip over the tin then thread a running stitch along the cast-on edge and gently pull tight, allowing the edge to cover the lip of the tin. Secure and oversew the rim edge.

### Strap/Handle

Cast on 8 st. Work in moss stitch (also known as seed stitch) until the work measures 87cm (34¼in) or desired length. Cast off.

### Making up

With the main piece of work, sew up the side seams using plarn. Run a gathering stitch along the cast-on edge, drawing it up tight and securing firmly. Turn the top edge down so that the reversed stocking stitch forms a little rim (see detail) and stitch in place. Position the strap 3cm (1¼in) down inside the holder. Stitch firmly into place. Now attach the other end of the strap in the same way, opposite the end you have just attached. Insert an empty food tin into the holder and push it right down to the bottom. Then hold a hot iron against the base until the plastic has fused, making sure you have the baking parchment between the work and the iron all the time! When the plastic has cooled, you can remove the tin can. The base will then be hard so that the bottle holder will stand up unsupported.

### The finished piece

*The plastic bags I used for this piece were black on the inside and green on the outside. When knitted up, they give the piece a lovely textured look.*

# Hair Clip

## Materials:

Plarn in red and green – small amounts
Sewing needle and thread
Three small beads
Jewellery findings: Hair clip attachment

## Needles:

1 pair 2.75mm (UK 12; US 2) knitting needles

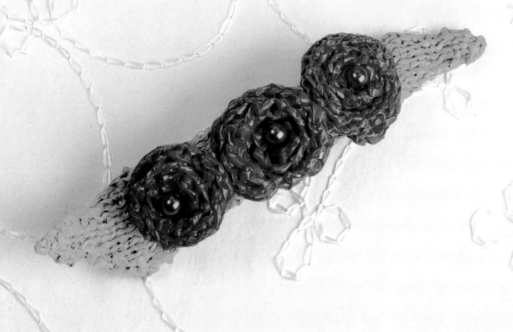

## Instructions:

### Knitting

### For the leaves

Cast on 5 st. Work 4 rows in stocking stitch ending on a purl row. Increase 1 stitch each end of the next row. Purl 1 row. Repeat the last 2 rows once more. Continue in stocking stitch straight for 10 rows, ending on a purl row. Decrease 1 stitch each end of the next row. Purl 1 row. Repeat the last 2 rows twice more (3 st remain). Stocking stitch 4 more rows. Cast off. Make two of these.

### For the roses

Cast on 4 st in red plarn. Work in stocking stitch until work measures 9cm (3½in) ending on a purl row. Next row decrease 1 stitch at the beginning then knit to end (2st remain). Continue in st st for another 3cm (1¼in). Cast off. Make three of these.

### Make up

Stitch the 2 leaves together along their cast-on edges. Sew in any unwanted ends of plarn. Now take the red knitting and, starting at the narrowest point, roll the work up, stitching it in place as you go to form a rose. When you have completed sewing all three roses, position and stitch them in place along the leaves. Sew the small beads into the centres of the roses with a fine sewing needle and thread (see detail opposite). Now you are ready to place the knitted flowers and leaves along the top of the hair clip attachment and stitch them securely in place.

## The finished piece

*I chose red roses for a romantic look, but pale colours have a nice summery feel.*

# Handbag

## Materials:

Plarn in purple, pink and lilac – approximately twenty standard-sized plastic bags

Darning needle

## Needles:

1 pair 3.75mm (UK 9; US 5) knitting needles

1 pair 2.75mm (UK 12; US 2) knitting needles

## Instructions:

### Knitting

The handbag is made in one piece as follows. Cast on 60 st. Work 6 rows in moss stitch (also known as seed stitch). Still in moss stitch knit 20 st, cast off 20 st, knit last 20 st. Next row moss stitch 20 st, cast on 20 st, knit the last 20 st. With these 60 st, work 15 rows in moss stitch. Next row work 20 st, cast off 20 st, and work last 20 st. Next row work 20 st, cast on 20 st, work last 20 st, resulting in 60 st again. Work 10 more rows in moss stitch.* Change to garter stitch and work 6 rows. Then 8 rows in stocking stitch.**

Repeat from * to ** until the work measures 22cm (8½in) from the start of the garter stitch. Work 10 rows in moss stitch; this forms the base of the bag. Return to knitting 6 rows of garter and 8 rows of stocking stitch until the work measures 22cm (8½in) from the moss stitch base. (There should be an equal number of rib and smooth stripes as knitted at the beginning.)

Work 10 rows of moss stitch. Next row work 20 st, cast off 20 st, work last 20 st. Next row work 20 st, cast on 20 st, work last 20 st. Work 15 rows in moss stitch. Next row work off 20 st, work last 20 st. Next row work 20 st, cast on 20 st, work last 20 st. Work another 6 rows in moss stitch. Cast off.

### For the roses

Make as roses for the Hair Clip (see page 39) but leaving off the hard bead in the centre. Make five of these.

### Making up

Sew in any unwanted ends of plarn. Fold the handles over so that the holes line up and they are double thickness. Oversew around the hand-hole, the sides and the inside edge. Do this also to the other end of the work. Now fold the bag in half so that the moss stitch strip is at the base and the handles join at the top. Oversew the sides of the bag together up to where the moss stitch handles start. This will leave a little vent for easier access. Position the roses along the first stocking stitch stripe of the bag and sew securely in place.

### The finished piece

*I have made a few handbags for special friends and they tell me they are regularly stopped and complimented on their gorgeous bags. They then tell the passer-by that the bag is made from recycled carrier bags and wait for the look of amazment!*

# Bangle

## Materials:

Plarn in ochre, cream and gold – approximately
  one carrier bag in each colour

Large plastic bangle

Darning needle

## Needles:

1 pair 2.75mm (UK 12; US 2) knitting needles

## Instructions:

### Knitting:
Cast on 15 st. Work in stocking stitch throughout. Work stripes as follows * 6 rows ochre, 2 rows cream, 4 rows gold, 2 rows ochre, 2 rows gold, 8 rows cream **. Repeat from * to ** until the work is long enough to cover the complete circumference of the bangle. Cast off.

### Making up
Stitch the two ends together to form a ring. Slip this over the bangle. Pull the sides of the knitting into the middle of the inside edge and stitch together, encasing the bangle in a knitted sleeve.

## Funky Bangle

*You can use your own imagination to make unique and personal pieces of jewellery. These are a favourite with my teenage children. Have fun!*

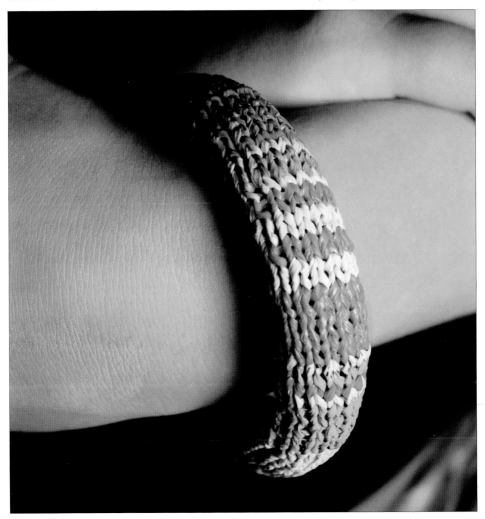

# Liquorice Jewellery

## Materials:

Plarn in white, black, pink, orange, yellow and blue – small amounts

Jewellery findings: one necklace clasp and two earring hooks

Seed beads in pale blue and pink

Approximately forty-two large black beads for separating the sweets

Darning and sewing needles and nylon thread

Sewing thread

## Needles:

1 pair 4mm (UK 8; US 6) knitting needles

## Necklace instructions:

Work all sweets in stocking stitch throughout.

### Three-layered sweets

**Knitting**

Cast on 5 st in white plarn and work 8 rows. Change to black plarn and work 9 more rows. Now join in the colour of your choice (pink, orange or yellow). Starting with a knit row on the wrong side of the work, work 8 rows. Cast off.

**Making up**

Sew in any unwanted ends then fold the white and black parts together with the right side of the stocking stitch on the outside.

Next, fold back the coloured part, again with the right side of the work visible. Stitch the piece together using matching coloured plarn. Make three of these.

### Black and white five-layered sweets

**Knitting**

Follow the instructions for the three-layered sweets, using only black and white plarn. Instead of casting off, work 9 rows in black, starting with a purl row. Change to white plarn for the last layer and work 8 rows. Cast off.

**Making up**

Fold together as for the three-layered sweets, plus the extra layers. Make two of these.

### Small pink and blue beaded sweets

**Knitting**

Using either pink or blue plarn, cast on 3 st and work in stocking stitch for 10cm (4in). Cast off.

**Making up**

This time with the back of work on show, roll the work up to form a small circular sweet. Stitch securely in place.

Using a sewing needle and thread, cover the whole sweet in seed beads that match in colour. Make two sweets in blue and one in pink.

### Circular sweets with black centres

**Knitting**

Cast on 3 st in black plarn and work 8 rows. Change to coloured plarn (pink, orange or yellow) and continue until the work measures 25cm (9¾in) or until the coloured part is long enough to wrap around the black centre 3 times when rolled up. Cast off.

**Making up**

Sew in any unwanted ends. Roll the work up starting with the black part, thus making a wheel shape. Stitch together to hold in place. Make three of these.

### Black and white cylinder-shaped sweets

**Knitting**

Cast on 5 st in white plarn and work 10 rows. Change to black plarn and work 14 rows, or just enough to cover the white centre once rolled up. Cast off. Make two of these.

**Making up**

Sew in any unwanted ends. Starting at the white end of the work, roll up until the white centre is completely wrapped in the black work and stitch in place.

**Making up the necklace**

Thread the sweets on to a nylon wire alternating each with a large black bead.

Use as many large beads as you need for the desired length at either end of the nylon thread. Knot the necklace clasp on either end firmly.

## Earring instructions:

### Knitting
Make two small beaded sweets and two circular sweets with black centres, as for the necklace.

### Making up
Thread two sweets on to nylon thread, alternating with black beads as shown to the left.

Make sure the sweets and beads are secure then thread and stitch them on to the earring attachment. Repeat for the second earring.

## Publishers' Note

If you would like more information on knitting techniques,
try the *Beginner's Guide to Knitting* by Alison Dupernex,
Search Press, 2004.